CHOICES
THE RON JAMES STORY

"LESSONS LEARNED FROM A REPEAT OFFENDER"

WORKBOOK
with Moral Concepts and Analyses

Choices — Workbook

Copyright 2018 by Ronald L. James

All rights reserved. No part of this book may be used or reproduced by any means, graphic, electronic, or mechanical, including photocopying, recording, taping or by any information storage retrieval system without the written permission of the author except in the case of brief quotations embodied in critical articles and reviews. This workbook is intended for use in partnership with the movie *Choices – Lessons Learned From A Repeat Offender*. If used as a companion to the book of the same name the sequence of events may appear in a different order.

ISBN: 978-1-945169-10-6

Published in Partnership with
Your Choice Publication
1245 Princess St.
York, PA 17404
717 850-3538
www.YourChoiceFoundation.org

&

Orison Publishers, Inc.
PO Box 188
Grantham, PA 17027
717 731-1405
www.OrisonPublishers.com

DEDICATION

First and foremost, I would like to dedicate this study guide to my loving wife and children, network of family and the friends who have helped me along my journey, and ultimately enabled me to reach out to inspire others. I would also like to thank the hundreds of thousands of parents, grandparents, guardians and individuals out there who have family or friends who have shared similar stories as mine, and to all of those who are still suffering and are searching for answers.

CONTENTS

Introduction viii
Problems 1
The Deal..3
Last Parole Visit..7
The James Family Home..11
School and Work Choices..15
Family Missteps..17
The LA Experience..21
Coke Stories 25
Coke Stories 2 27
Gypsy 31
Ron and Gypsy 35
First-Time Jailbird 37
Meeting Lindor and Finding Crack........................41
Meeting Kiss 45
Second-time Jailbird...49
Clocking..53
The Road Out of (And Back to) Jail 57
Third-time Jailbird 61
A Budding Author 63
Mimi's Passing and Ron's Chance 65

A Time for Reflection 67
An Unexpected Impact 69
Parole Board 71
Back to the World 73
The Helpers That Came 59
Parole Free 79
Conclusion 81

INTRODUCTION

Getting involved with drugs is exactly like going down the rabbit hole; finding your way back is a great feat and you're never truly the same if and when you do get back.

This workbook chronicles the experiences of Ronald L. James, a recovered drug addict and alcoholic and consequently, a person of multiple incarcerations. It is based on a script for a movie about his life released in 2018.

The original movie script is retold in summary fashion in this workbook. Commentary and questions are provided to aid the reader or study group in examining the events and perhaps even applying relevant lessons to their own lives.

It is the author's hope that this workbook impacts heavily upon the reader and leaves a lasting impression.

PROBLEMS

As the movie opens, we hear sirens, gunshots and barking dogs. A man, trying to elude capture, is running for his life. He breaks into a back door of a home. Crouching down and breathing heavily from the chase, he gingerly peers out the curtained pane thinking he may be safe. Suddenly we see a shotgun pointed to the back of his head as the homeowner glaringly questions what he is doing in her home.

The scene fades away to a couple in a car outside Philadelphia. This is our protagonist, Ron James. When we meet him he is not in the best shape of his life. He used to be a good-looking smooth talker, born salesman and ladies' man. At this point, he is none of those things, just a broken man with a strong addiction. He drives a beat-up old car that would fail every test of roadworthiness. Ron doesn't care. At least the car gets him wherever he needs to be and he usually only needs to be at one place — wherever the drugs are.

Sitting beside his shaky body in the passenger seat is a woman he calls his girl-friend. Her name is Princess D. The affection they both share is mostly superficial and doesn't compare in any way to the affection they have for getting high. As the car idles outside the home of a drug dealer, they finalize their plans to trade a new video camera for drugs since they have no money. Princess D is pleading for him to hurry as she needs her fix.

ANALYSIS
1. Based on the story line above, is it fair to say that drugs degrade a person's abilities? How can you tell?

2. Do you think that without their shared love of drugs, Ron and Princess D would typically have been friends?

3. How deeply do drugs appear to have a hold on Ron considering that he has to resort to trading electronic products to get his fix?

THE DEAL

Ron enters the drug dealer's home, carrying the concealed video camera, and is greeted by the owner, a man named Dino. He recognizes Ron and invites him to come in while asking if Ron has anything for him. Ron shows him the new video camera, which he brought along for the trade. Dino accepts the camera and wonders aloud that Ron must have a warehouse full of electronics.

As Ron walks further into the room, he sees the remnants of a drug party. Most of the people left behind, lying around the room, are still high on something, but Ron isn't too concerned with them. His focus is on the fix and he is annoyed that Dino doesn't appear ready for the quick trade.

After a brief moment of apprehension he follows Dino, as instructed, into the adjacent bedroom, to finish the deal. After fumbling around for the product, Dino claims to have forgotten something and exits the room, telling Ron to wait there. Left alone in the room Ron is almost certain he's been lured into a trap.

As he hears a crash and a scream he rushes back into the front room. Dino's men have dragged Princess D into the house and have thrown her onto the floor. Dino is nowhere to be seen. An altercation breaks out between Ron and the men but he is quickly outnumbered and overpowered. Knocking him to the ground, they continue to kick him until he is spitting blood.

The door opens again. This time it's Dino and he calls off his men. The men then show Dino the treasure trove of goods they found in Ron's trunk - a briefcase filled with hundreds of checks and credit applications. Princess D cries to them not to take it, pleading that their entire lives are in there. Dino now taunts Ron and Princess D, inviting *them* to call the cops. Seemingly now irritated by their presence, he throws a bag of crack on the floor telling them to get out - that they got what they came for.

MORAL CONCEPT:

At this point we have observed two scenarios in Ron's life that represent poor choices, that have placed him in difficult situations. Choices that have been made without the context of moral standards. In this workbook we will introduce some of the more common moral concepts and examine how they relate to the storyline. Morals are typically defined as standards of behavior or beliefs concerning what is acceptable and what is not, or simply what is right or wrong. Some may call this a code of ethics, principles or values. For our purpose we will call them morals. A short list of morals might include Honesty, Responsibility, Self Discipline, Friendship, Compassion, Courage, Perseverance, and Work Ethic. Developing these traits helps anchor us, providing the stability and direction we need in navigating life.

ANALYSIS:

1. Is there anything you would add to the above list of morals? Which ones do you think are in question in these first two scenarios?

2. How familiar do you think the relationship is between Ron and Dino? What have you observed about this?

3. When Ron walked in to purchase the drugs, he felt something was off. Why do you think he just didn't walk away?

4. What can you infer from Dino's convenient absence as his men attacked Ron and stole the documents from the trunk of his car?

5. Think back to when Dino threw the bag of crack at Ron while he was writhing on the floor in pain. What can you deduce from this action about the way Dino regards Ron? Can you infer anything from this incident about the general relationship between drug dealers and drug addicts?

6. At one point, Dino mockingly suggests they call the police if they wish. Seeing as Dino himself is engaged in criminal behavior, do you find this ironic?

LAST PAROLE VISIT

Fifteen years later, we see Ron James in his parole officer's office as he makes his final visit. His parole officer, Rick shows him a box filled with file folders containing Ron's criminal records. Rick calls them "The Criminal Exploits of Ronald L. James."

Both men discuss some of the criminal actions detailed in those folders and then Rick pulls out the folder which intrigued him the most. It's a folder documenting Ron's violations of his current parole and it is has remained *empty*. Rick shares how remarkable this is as so many paroles continually return to jail, yet Ron has stayed clean.

When Rick asks Ron how he managed to do it, the answer is simple. "Choices",

Ron says. "When I make good choices I stay out of jail. When I make bad choices I go back in."

MORAL CONCEPT:
One of the first moral concepts we will discuss is Responsibility, which represents the ability to act independently and to make decisions on our own. But it also implies *taking care of* the things we are charged with and for *being accountable* for them, whether it is for ourselves, family, a task or a job. Taking responsibility for things is a concept we typically see only in mature individuals. Yet it can be practiced daily in so many ways. We become who we are by the very decisions and choices that we make each day to carry out our given responsibilities. We can do it with dignity and honor, or we can be irresponsible and selfish, caring only for our self and our own needs, and making unwise choices. The decision is always *ours* to make. This is the lesson that Ron ultimately learned, but as you will

observe, it did not come without effort and significant personal cost. The choices we make become our way of life.

ANALYSIS:

1. What do the multiple files suggest about Ron's criminal life?

2. Why do you think Rick was so intrigued by the *empty* folder in Ron's file?

3. Do you think that a thing as simple as "choices" can determine whether an individual ends up in jail or not? Share your thoughts about this.

4. Have you ever neglected any of your responsibilities, minor or major?

THE JAMES FAMILY HOME

A flashback takes us back to the 60s, where we see the home of matriarch, Mimi James. It is evident that she is a strong, caring woman and that she showers her affection on her young son, Ron. She's also a tough woman, but early on, Ron finds a way to bypass his mother's toughness. When he is caught fighting with another boy and is reprimanded by Mimi, he says that he was fighting because the boy called her a bad name. Instead of being scolded, his actions now were viewed as honorable.

Ron continues to experiment with making bad choices and one day, he throws a large rock sized walnut at the head of a police officer standing a short distance away. As his friends run off, he stands his ground as the officer confronts him, announcing that he is in big trouble. Ron quickly makes another bad choice - to lie in hopes of being let off easy. He formulates a story about his mother being ill and how it would impact her health even more if he were to get into trouble. It works like a charm and Ron begins to believe that he can easily manipulate people, and as such, bypass the consequences of his actions.

Even though he is now beginning to feel invincible, a little voice, his conscience, wells up inside him, asking him what he is doing. He looks down at the cracked sidewalk and sees a small stinkbug on that sidewalk. This triggers a painful early memory when Ron was reading aloud in front of his classmates at school. As he struggled over each word the other children laughed at him. Humiliated, Ron slipped back into his seat and put his head down, vowing to never read again. Part of the storyline he was trying to read included a reference to a stinkbug.

At the time, Ron doesn't realize it, but the cracked sidewalk was a metaphor for his life - a good life that he allowed bad things to take root in. Naturally, these bad things would cause a lot of damage in his life.

MORAL CONCEPT:

This episode strongly depicts the moral of Honesty, or specifically the lack of it. At a very early age, Ron experimented with a simple lie and as he got away with it, he moved on to more lies. It became a way of life for him, and he became quite good at deceiving others. The core definition of honesty includes the words sincere, free from deceit and untruthfulness, morally correct or virtuous. It is also associated with these strong words: integrity, ethical, positive, honorable, fair, trustworthy, sincere, truthful, straightforward, incorruptible. When you read these words, how do they make you feel. Would these characteristics draw you to other people who exhibited them? Would these same traits draw others to you if you exhibited them? Honesty is a character trait that is well worth developing. Not only is it moral, but it's very presence in your life demonstrates that you have self respect and that you respect others. Dishonesty suggests the exact opposite. Honesty is open and thrives in light, whereas dishonesty is secretive, deceptive and thrives in darkness. Our conscience may be considered a sort of moral faculty that attempts to keep us on the right course, but in order for it to guide us, we have to first have a clear understanding of what is right and what is wrong.

ANALYSIS:

1. What have you observed about Mimi's parenting style? Was it in any way responsible for Ron's actions? Was he making those choices on his own?

2. How may these early experiences with lying (and acting) have shaped his thinking?

3. Should the policeman have let him off so easy? Should he have believed Ron's story? Would you?

4. After his classmates laughed at him, how do you think Ron should have reacted? What's another choice he could have made? How could the teacher have intervened?

5. Were these events significant in shaping and influencing the person he would become?

6. Regarding the inner voice Ron heard - would you characterize that as the internal conflict between what is right and wrong? Do you think we are all guided by an inner voice or conscience? Has yours ever prompted you to question your actions?

SCHOOL AND WORK CHOICES

Ron continues to hate reading, and doesn't pick up another book for 12 more years. He becomes a major manipulator. In order to pass exams in school he chooses -wrongly again - to become a master at cheating. He cheats his way through the rest of his school days, even into college, which ultimately leads to his expulsion. Ron then lands a good job working on a shipping dock, but can't let go of his cheating habit. He considers the job to be too much "work" and one day while pulling a heavy load off a truck, he falls to the ground and feigns pain in his back. As others rush to his aid, he smiles to himself, seeing that his "trick" worked. Soon he is receiving checks from workers' compensation, happy once again to have cheated the system.

MORAL CONCEPT:
Consider how the morals of Responsibility and Honesty apply here as well. What respect was Ron showing to his teachers, and classmates when he cheated, and to his boss and co-workers when he cheated at work later, or just as importantly, to himself? His poor choices are setting the stage for more hardship, but he is oblivious to that at this point. Aristotle once wrote that good habits formed at youth make all the difference. Ron apparently did not learn these habits early on, and as a result made repeated questionable choices during his youth and young adult years.

ANALYSIS:
1. What do you think Aristotle meant? Do you think it is too late for Ron at this point?

2. Do you know people who depend on cheating to get ahead in any aspect of life? What do you think of their actions?

3. What have you observed about Ron's work habits? Did old habits follow him to the workplace?

4. How successful is Ron likely to be in future jobs with this type of work ethic?

FAMILY MISSSTEPS

The people in Ron's family - the men specifically - have a long-standing romance with crime and bad behavior, having taken on professions such as bank robbers, drug dealers and con-men. One of these relatives, Marvin, soon reaches out to Ron. He is Ron's cousin and he is fresh out of jail. He tells Ron that he has a great plan to make lots of cash and that they should get together to discuss this.

When they finally meet, Marvin spins a tale regarding how his brother, Tyrone, had been making millions selling drugs all over the city. He suggests that he and Ron team up and start dealing, calling it "independent capitalism."

Ron hesitates for a moment, and points out that Tyrone had eventually been gunned down at a nightclub. Marvin replies that a thing like that would never happen to them. He is confident that when they get the drugs, he and Ron will be able to move them around efficiently and that they will restore the family to its "former glory." Ron considers this, and ultimately, his answer to the offer is an affirmative yes.

MORAL CONCEPTS:
Think back to what Aristotle said about the value of good habits being formed at a young age. For young people to develop morals and values, these things must be illustrated by example through watching others, or taught through learning or reading. We all need to learn to discern right from wrong and good from bad behaviors. This serves as a moral compass to guide us. Imagine living in a world without morals, values or a conscience, where there were no guidelines or standards. How would we know our water was safe to drink, or medications safe to take when we are sick, or how safe our money would be when we deposit funds in a bank. How would schools,

business and medical facilities function without rules or standards? What would be the outcome?

ANALYSIS:

1. Can you imagine the chaos that would occur if there were no rules or standards in life, or in the world? What would that look like? How would things get done? How would decisions be made?

2. In your opinion, are we limited by circumstances beyond our control, such as upbringing or family influence for example? Although circumstance may create opportunity - whether good or bad - do you believe it is our free will to ultimately make our own choices regarding our actions?

3. When Ron heard Marvin say on the phone that he had a plan to get them "lots of cash", do you think he should have been wary?

4. Why do you think Ron eventually agreed to go along with Marvin's scheme?

THE LA EXPERIENCE

Ron and Marvin fly to Los Angeles where Marvin has drug connections. The dealer they intend to meet has a large home and both men arrive there in a cab.

They pay cash for the drugs and the dealer shows them how to "make work" out of it. He shows them how to safely transport the stash and how to cut it so they can make even more profits. Even after cutting, they realize they would be selling the highest quality cocaine in Philadelphia. Both men are pleased with this. They plan to stay over for a few nights before their return flight.

Ron, who initially considered this dealer to be rock solid, begins to sense that something is a little off. That night, Ron is restless and hears loud static noise from the living room. Puzzled by the sound, he walks cautiously into the room. He sees the dealer cowering in fear, watching his home security feed on a large TV screen as it frantically whips from room to room. Ron tries to ask a question but the dealer, acting terrified, hushes him. Ron fears that someone - maybe the police - are onto them and when he asks the dealer, he again hushes Ron, whispering, "They are listening to us", as he furtively looks all around the room. Soon the dealer passes out on the sofa.

As Ron shares this strange encounter with Marvin the next morning they both realize that their dealer is also a hard core user. As they make plans to return home, Marvin shares "That's why I don't touch the product". However, Ron's curiosity is heightened. He begins to wonder about the pleasure coke users derive from using the drug. As a heavy alcohol user, he feels invincible to its effects and makes the assumption that he would have a similar tolerance to these stronger drugs.

MORAL CONCEPT:

Consider here the moral of Honest Work. One definition suggests work is to simply achieve a purpose or a result - to accomplish something. It can be mental or physical. Work that is most valued is something that achieves a *worthy* purpose, and certainly one that does not cause harm to others. Much is written about the pleasure received from doing meaningful work and having a positive impact on others. Even in menial types jobs, there is honor in doing the job well and with dignity. It's been said that there aren't any menial jobs, only menial attitudes. Ron perceived his job on the dock to be beneath him, and looked for shortcuts to doing an honest day's work. Though the work he found with Marvin may turn a quick dollar, it was illegal, immoral, and the cause of much suffering to others - and perhaps even causing loss of life. It is fair to say he was not operating with a good moral compass.

ANALYSIS:
1. Do you think Ron is proud of the kind of work he is doing?

2. In your opinion, what do you think accounted for the dealer's strange behavior the night Ron encountered him in the living room?

2. What might Marvin have known about the stronghold of these drugs, that Ron was not aware of? Why wouldn't he have shared more about that? What might that signal about Marvin's true concern for Ron?

3. Why do you think Ron chose to ignore the soft advice that Marvin did share that he never touches the product?

COKE STORIES

Ron soon begins to travel to small towns to make drug deliveries. While in his hotel room, with nothing to do, he considers the packet of cocaine sitting on the night table beside the bed. He hears a tempting voice say to him, "Go ahead Ron, you can handle it. Have a little fun for once." As he picks it up, his voice of reason begins to tell him it's a bad idea. He is reminded of the side effects, which could include addiction and becoming a "dope fiend". Feeling invincible, Ron disregards this voice, telling himself that he's special and that things like addiction do not happen to people like him. He manages to convince himself of this and in the end, he snorts the packet of coke.

MORAL CONCEPT:
Ron's actions here are faulty in so many ways. He is being irresponsible with materials that are not his, literally stealing from his own partner or employer, Marvin. He is being irrational in believing that he would magically be immune to the effects of drugs, and he ignores his conscience. The moral that comes to mind is Accountability. Webster defines this as the state of being answerable for something within your power, control or management; being the person who caused something to happen; or a duty or task that you are required or expected to do because it is morally right or legally required. His life right now is like a train that is heading into a very long and dark tunnel.

ANALYSIS:
1. Do you think Ron's relationship with alcohol aided his decision to try cocaine?

2. Now that he has tried snorting coke, do you think he will be able to turn away from it at will?

3. Does Ron seem to be in control of his life at this point, or is something else driving his decisions?

4. When he was in these small towns, bored, and contemplating using the product how could he have managed this situation differently?

COKE STORIES 2

Later that night, Ron realizes the coke packet is empty and begins to panic. It's very clear what has happened but he is hesitant to tell Marvin the truth. Ron thinks he has to come up with a foolproof story. Finally, he calls Marvin and tells him that he's never going to believe what happened: that he "spilled the candy on a shag carpet." A seemingly unending moment of silence passes, but in the end Marvin says, "No problem. We don't sweat the crumbs." Ron feels great that he's able to get away with the deceit and at that moment, he goes officially from dealer to his own best customer.

MORAL CONCEPT:
Let's consider the moral responsibility to be responsible means to be accountable for your actions; to live up to a code of established ethics. You'll do what you say you're going to do, and you're honest and fair, even trustworthy. Was Ron any of these things with Marvin? And now he is lying to him as well. Have you ever heard the term "like begets like"? It frequently is used to infer a strong similarity that exists between parents and offspring. But it is not also true that we are influenced by those we choose to spend time with? We become what we surround ourselves with; what we read, what we see and what we listen to. All these things have a significant impact or influence on who we are and what we become. The social norms and values of the drug world will likely become Ron's norms and values simply by association. He is embarking on a very slippery slope.

ANALYSIS:
1. What are the things that surround you that influence your life?

2. Do you think Marvin believed Ron's story about what happened to the delivery? Share your opinion why or why not?

3. What do you think about Ron's aptitude for lying? Do you think it got him out of trouble, just like he believed? Or, do you think it just gave him a false sense of confidence?

4. Can you think of a serious situation where you attempted to lie? How did you feel about it? Did it cause you great worry for fear of being found out? Was it ultimately worth it?

5. What books, music and life or street education is impacting your life? Are these forces beneficial or harmful to you? Are there elements of influence in your life you should reconsider?

GYPSY

In this scene, Ron and Marvin visit George to collect money owed to them. George has no money and offers to pay them some other way. He introduces them to his cousin, "Gypsy", proclaiming she can "solve all their problems." Gypsy confirms that they could help *her* make some money. When Marvin asks what kind of business she is in, she simply answers, "Profiles." This clicks with Ron, and he goes to his car to retrieve the profiles from earlier work he had done with dating services. He presents these to Gypsy, allowing her to review them. She shares she will need to do a test run; if the profiles are good, she'll pay them five hundred dollars up front.

With Marvin doubting the success of her methods, Gypsy instructs George to give him a VCR for a down payment on what he still owes. She reassures them that George will work off the balance owed them, and that she will be in touch. Ron soon discovers that Gypsy has a legendary reputation in Philadelphia as an "entrepreneur" who can sell anything she can get her hands on. However her preferred scam is to take personal information, prepare fake checks and impersonate victims long enough to withdraw funds from their bank accounts.

She is willing to teach Ron, and initially takes him on as a driver. After pulling off several jobs, Ron wants a larger role and convinces Gypsy to let him make the withdrawals. After teaching him how it works and coaching him on which type of bank teller to avoid, Gypsy allows Ron a test run. He is successful in withdrawing the funds and they continue working as a team.

MORAL CONCEPT:
Once again, Responsibility, Honesty and Self-Discipline all come to mind here. Ron is getting in deeper as his circle widens and his street education is expanding in ways that will cause him even greater harm.

ANALYSIS:

1. Consider the old saying " Crime never pays". Do you believe that to be true?

2. Why do you think Ron got involved in the identity theft scheme? Why didn't Marvin? What factors may have driven each of their decisions?

3. Do you believe Ron was feeling the Midas touch - that all he touched was golden, and that his luck would continue to hold out?

4. What is your impression Gypsy? Is she the kind of business partner you would want to work with?

RON AND GYPSY

Ultimately Ron marries Gypsy with Mimi's full support of their union. Ron has an abundance of money at this point and things seem to be going well. One day, as they park their car outside their home, an acquaintance of Ron's nervously approaches them. He alerts Ron that his house has been under surveillance all week, and that even now there is a car watching him right down the street. Ron thanks him while Gypsy slips quietly into the house. Ron exits his car and begins casually walking away from the house.

At this point, the unmarked police car approaches him, and the driver calls out to Ron by name. Ron initially pretends to be someone else, but as they persist, he senses trouble and takes off running. A foot chase begins. Ron loses the officers for a while but is apprehended then he runs into a dead end.

ANALYSIS

1. What values do you think Ron and Gypsy's marriage was based on?

2. Could overconfidence have played a role in Ron's downfall? Was it just meant to happen? Why?

3. At this point in the story, do you think crime pays?

FIRST-TIME JAILBIRD

Ron lands in jail for the first time and he is stunned. Bail is denied and he remains there for nine long months. He quickly learns that part of the unwritten prison code is that whoever is in the cell first makes all the rules. His cellmate promptly tells him exactly where he may and *may not* sit and sleep, and even demands that he always remove his shoes while in the cell. After learning his cellmate was convicted of murder, Ron is careful to watch his every step.

Later when Ron is released, he relishes the freedom outside of the prison walls. All too soon he craves the high that he thought he had forgotten. Within a single day, he turns back to crack, and as always, he needs money to fund it. His bank accounts have already been emptied by attorney fees and court costs. He rushes over to Gypsy's house and discovers Gypsy and "her people" have helped themselves to all his possessions, including his secret money stash. It is apparent that Gypsy values cocaine over her relationship with Ron. He decides he is now through with her.

Still needing money for his next high, Ron begins a new scam ripping off clothing stores with fake checks and pocketing the difference. He even returns to the same store twice, despite knowing that it is never wise to return to the scene of a crime.

MORAL CONCEPTS:
Through the years to come, Ron will often return to jail. On each occasion he met with different cellmates. In one situation he found himself with a rather vicious looking inmate who took pleasure in ordering him around. Tensions were high and things could have escalated at any time. The situation was diffused when his cellmate was placed in solitary confinement, and Ron was spared from a potentially dangerous situation and physical assault. How did he ever end up in this situation?

Choices is one answer. And perhaps it begins with the choice of friends. Another moral is Friendship. True friendship is when individuals really care for the well-being of one another. It's defined as a mutual state of trust and support, a friendly feeling or attitude, a kindness or help given to someone. On the other hand, a counterfeit friendship is one that focus more on selfishness, such as the Ron's friendship with Gypsy and others before her. The selection of our friends, and who we spent time with is of critical importance - because they have a strong influence on who we become. The good ones can make us better, while the bad ones help to drag us down to their level.

ANALYSIS:

1. Have you even had a counterfeit friend? Would you know if you did?

2. Who are your friends and colleagues? Are they a positive force in your life? Do they help you to become a better person? Or do they pull you down to their level?

3. How do you think Ron felt upon his release when he found he had been "cleaned out" of all his money and possessions by his own wife? Was the basis of their relationship real love or was it a counterfeit relationship?

4. Why do you think Ron chose to seek solace in drugs again, after his release?

5. What could have motivated Ron to start up new scams? Do you wonder about his choices? What, if any, other choices might have been available to him?

6. How difficult do you think it is to change the patterns you have become familiar and perhaps even comfortable with in your life?

7. What role models did Ron have in his life that helped shape his morals and life choices?

MEETING LINDOR AND FINDING CRACK

Ron begins seeing a lot of women after Gypsy and becomes particularly enamored by a young girl named Lindor. She is always welcoming to Ron, and to the drugs he brings. Her specialty is cooking the powder into a rock and smoking it. She asks Ron if he's ever smoked the pipe before. When Ron remains silent, she tempts him until he agrees to try.

That was the first night Ron smoked with a glass pipe, and from that moment on that was all he ever wanted. He refers to crack as his "Maggie May" - from the lyrics of the Rod Stewart song - *"you stole my soul, and that's a pain I could live without"*. He shares how being called a crack head on the streets is ultimately hitting the bottom of the barrel, and that was exactly where he soon found himself. He had sunk to a new low.

(Though not shown in the movie, Ron began at this time to regularly visit crack houses.

Nothing deterred him from patronizing them, not the numerous fights or stick-ups and surely not the several stabbings and shootings. At the crack houses, he saw people stand still for hours in a daze. Some mutilated themselves; others jumped out of windows. The crack houses smelled badly; roaches and rats were regular tenants. If you were not high, the smell could knock you out cold but Ron was such a part of the whole process that at times the smell was coming from him. Personal cleanliness, basic responsibilities to self and others, even eating, all took a back seat to the quest for another fix. It consumed all thoughts. Like many others in that situation, he only lived for that "next" high.)

Ron's crack habit needs to be fed daily, so each day he tries to find a way to get money. He begins to exchange electronics for drugs, conspires with shady store owners to get insurance money and even robs himself to get insurance payments. On one occasion he is so desperate, he puts a pair of pliers in his pocket, pretends it's a gun and robs a store for crack money. Every dollar went to the same place - to his dealer for that next fix.

The scene flashes back to the parole office, where Ron is meeting with his parole officer, Rick. He asks Ron how he could get in such a position when it was clear how drugs were destroying people every day. Ron replies that his problem was chasing the high of that first hit; though he tried many different drugs and varying amounts he was never able to replicate that first high. It was elusive yet it called to him constantly. It was a day and night struggle to fight the need for that next hit - a need that was as compelling to him as the need to *breathe*.

MORAL CONCEPTS
Patterns are hard to break and Ron continues to make bad choices in his life. As he forges ahead now on his own, his life becomes even less his own, as his addiction now steers his every action. It is like a parasite, that hangs onto its host, selfishly robbing him of all that he has and then attacking his very health. If you have ever encounteredtemptation then you know the stronghold it can take in an individual's life. One course of action is to avoid those situations where temptation exists. Ron however continued to think he was invincible, and placed himself directly in the path of harm's way. Is it possible he may have also been impacted by the desire to "be cool" or to even impress Lindor?

ANALYSIS:

1. Think about Ron's relationship with Lindor. Does she seem more interested in Ron as a person, or in the drugs he brings to her?

2. Does there seem to be a pattern or common thread in Ron's relationship with the women in his life (Princess D, Gypsy, Lindor)? Do you think this is obvious to him at this stage in his life?

3. At this point in his life Ron knew the effects of smoking crack. Why then did he accept Lindor's offer to smoke it?

4. Ron tells his parole office that he always kept trying to replicate the high of that first hit. Could this be one reason why addictions have such a hold on individuals? What may be other reasons?

MEETING KISS

Ron soon meets a new dealer named Kiss, a young, charming sort of guy for a dealer. By this point, Ron realizes that a lot of dealers treat addicts like "sub-human garbage" but Kiss is respectful and Ron values that in him.

Very late one night, after 1:15 a.m., Ron finds himself in a difficult situation and calls Kiss to ask if he has a gun. Ron explains that the girl he came to the bar with has set him up and that there are guys waiting on him outside. He needs to be taken out of there fast. When Kiss pulls up in his car, he recognizes the men and knows they're not playing games. Kiss's reputation and protection allows Ron to be safely escorted to the car.

Back in the car, Kiss reflects on the events of the evening and his own risk in coming to Ron's aid. He shares his own story, telling Ron that he wasn't always on the corner dealing; he once had dealers and several crack houses under him. He was even signed to a label. Eventually, his dealers got busted, his stashes robbed and he had to start hustling deals on the streets himself. He shares how ironically this all began after his mother, a former addict, "found Jesus and began to pray" for him. He started to lose everything, because in his words, "Jesus is looking out for me". Ron tells him not to worry and that he'll bring him in on a future job. We soon learn that both Ron and Kiss end up in jail.

MORAL CONCEPT:
Compassion is one of the morals worthy of mention. It is defined as empathy, sympathy, a concern or support for others in need. It can take on many forms and shapes - from nurturing, tenderness, mercy, warmth, love, kindness, love, concern, tolerance, encouragement, or even charity. Without compassion in our lives, we can wither and become shells of our former selves. While they showed some signs of

compassion to one another, both Ron and Kiss had turned their backs to family that had their best interests at heart, and instead surrounded themselves with similarly empty shelled, self absorbed acquaintances, headed toward nowhere.

ANALYSIS:
1. Why would you think that drug dealers in general might treat drug users/addicts like "sub-human garbage"?

2. What would make Kiss risk personal harm to come to Ron's rescue that night?

3. Why would Kiss believe that his mother's prayers were actually causing him harm?

4. What would possibly motivate either Ron or Kiss to now plan a "robbery"?

SECOND-TIME JAILBIRD

The scene opens to Ron in the jail's exercise yard. He notices a young new arrival and observes that he looks a little frightened in his new surroundings. Ron proceeds to introduce himself to Nathanial and offers him a few tips on survival in jail. Later back in his cell, Ron meets his new cellmate, Dwight. As they scope each other out Dwight appears relieved to learn that Ron is not doing time for murder. Dwight boasts that he is only in jail because he got caught and that he will "do better" next time.

In a voice-over Ron shares how typical it is for inmates to say they are never coming back to prison. He shares that many will proclaim to family and friends how much they have changed. Others profess to having found God, which Ron indicates was true in his case. He acknowledges his belief that he is finally ready to get his life back on track.

The scene changes to Ron's release date and we see him walking out of jail. He briefly sees a vision of Maggie May waiting there for him on the corner. He hesitates for a moment, then a knowing smile creeps onto his face, and we fear he will pick up right where he left off. True to form, he returns to his lifestyle of drug use just one day after his release.

MORAL CONCEPT:
Here we see evidence of Compassion, as Ron attempts to help put a young man at ease in a new situation. We also see lack of Self-Discipline as we see Ron slip back into old patterns so soon after he is released.

ANALYSIS:

1. What might have led Ron to helping out the young inmate Nathaniel on his first day of imprisonment?

2. Reflect on Dwight's proclamation that he will do better next time. What do you think he means by that? What would be your prediction for his success when he is released? What is your prediction for Ron?

3. Are you surprised by how quickly Ron picks up right where he left off with "Maggie May" upon his release?

4. When an inmate leaves jail, consider the challenges they face with finding lodging, a job, their next meal, and all that is associated with getting re-acclimated to the outside world. Would you think this is a difficult task?

CLOCKING

One of the ways Ron had obtained money for drugs is a scheme called "clocking". This involves approaching someone at a stoplight or intersection to tell a false tale of having a broken down car and needing cash for repairs.

In this scene Ron, and a colleague he introduces as his girlfriend, use this scheme not once, but twice on a trusting and naïve college coed, Sally. Initially Ron pretends to only need $40. He portrays that the money would just be a quick loan that he will *definitely* pay back.

Sally meets the need with cash, and even shares her phone number and address in case they have any further problems. Ron calls her the next day, still under a false persona and reminds her of her help the previous night. She asks if his car is now fixed. Ron indicates no, that his wallet is still halfway across town and they still need $150 more for the repairs.

Sally volunteers to loan him even more cash that he can pay back when he gets home. When Ron tries to act like he doesn't want to be a bother, Sally tells him that her daddy told her to treat people in need like they were Jesus himself. She invites Ron and his "girlfriend" to come to her dorm room to pick up the funds.

On arrival he produces a fake payroll check, asking her to cash it as payment for the loan and to take the difference, because she was so nice to them. The still trusting Sally shares how that isn't necessary that she will bring the change right back to them. She leaves them in her room with her roommate as she runs off to the nearby bank.

The scene now changes to a hotel room, where Ron is experiencing a nightmarish "high". He is crouched in the corner of the room looking around in paranoia. He sees multiple demons in his mind and physically battles them. Later, exhausted and coming down from the drugs, he stumbles into the bathroom. The man he sees in the mirror is a mess. At the sight, Ron falls to the floor and begins to cry out to God.

Later that day, still haunted by this bad experience and feeling remorseful about how he had taken advantage of Sally, Ron calls her. He tells her his real name and confesses that he has conned her. Sally expresses confusion with his story because she believes she *was* paid back in full. Ron tells her that the check probably hasn't gone through the system, again apologizing. Somewhat shaken at the realization that her goodwill was taken for granted, and her money is now gone, Sally simply says, "May God bless you, Sir" and ends the call. The scene closes on a broken Ron looking upward.

MORAL CONCEPT:

The moral in question here would certainly be Honesty. A life that is built on deceit and dishonesty will not last forever. It will crumble. Friendships that are centered on selfishness and shared drug habits are not true friendships. Ron experiences a breakthrough moment when he sees what he has become and his conscience grabs a hold of him, however briefly.

ANALYSIS:

1. How easy do you think it would it be to fall victim to a clocking scam? What if anything, might make it seem believable?

2. What factors contributed to Ron scamming Sally more than once?

3. What could have been responsible for Ron's decision to call Sally to apologize for what he did? Do you believe he was truly remorseful? If so, why?

4. What transpired in Ron's experience with his "bad high"? Do you think he ever expected that could happen to him?

5. When he broke down after looking at himself in the mirror, did you think this might signal the end of his addiction, or would Ron continue on the same path?

THE ROAD OUT OF (AND BACK TO) JAIL

When Ron leaves jail this time, one of the first things he does is get married again. This time it's to the lovely Latanya Moore. Things go well for some time but Ron still has a crack habit and it affects his job, and his marriage. Ron loses his job, and later becomes enraged with Latanya when he sees her laughing on her cell phone. Thinking she is cheating on him, he uses this as an excuse to tear the house apart, take her money and then leave. From this point forward, his crack habit, once again, takes priority in his life. Even later, when Latanya is at the hospital giving birth, Ron is absent.

We next see Ron fleeing a convenience store that he just robbed. The owner races out of the store after him, firing off several shots. A bullet whizzes past Ron's ears but he manages to escape, ducking behind a car. He realizes that he is risking his life for his habit, but even that doesn't stop him from continuing to make bad choices, and ultimately he again finds himself in a courtroom.

As we hear the distinctive pound of a gavel, we see Ron being sentenced once again. His mother, Mimi, appears to be the only person there for him, and as he is led him away, in her deep sorrow, she forms the silent words "I love you".

She visits him in jail, though in ill health, and asks rhetorically where she went wrong. Ron tells her not to blame herself and apologizes for always letting her down. She tries to encourage him by telling him to keep his head up.

MORAL CONCEPT:
We have previously defined the moral of Responsibility. This certainly comes to mind as we look at Ron's marriage. He was unable to hold onto his job, to manage his temper and to provide for his wife and child in the

way he should. Was Ron in control of his decisions at this time or was something else in control? Ultimately you could say it was his choice to allow that. Would you agree with that statement?

ANALYSIS:

1. How well did Ron live up to his responsibilities in his marriage? Do you think Latanya was aware of Ron's crack habit before she married him? How might an addiction like this impact a marriage?

2. Ron had all the same responsibilities we all have to be law abiding citizens. Yet he continually throws that off and steps into questionable behaviors to feed his selfish desires. What do you think about how his activities have now escalated to robbery?

3. How do you think Ron felt when that bullet whizzed by his head, narrowly missing him? Would an event like that convince you to change your ways? Why was that not enough to convince Ron?

4. Why do you believe Mimi was the only person to attend Ron's sentencing and to later visit him in jail?

5. How could Ron's imprisonment impact Mimi, Latanya, or their daughter?

THIRD-TIME JAILBIRD

While Ron in jail playing chess with an inmate, a TV news report catches his attention. It details a shooting at a convenience store where the shopkeeper killed a robber. When the front of the store is shown Ron recognizes the store as the same one he had robbed. He remembers how he felt when the bullet passed his ear and again realizes how lucky he was. He hears his chess partner say to him, "That could have been you."

Next we see Nathaniel, the young man Ron gave advice to on his first day in jail, stopping by Ron's cell. He invites him to a Bible Study. Ron declines, saying that he doesn't like reading, but Nathaniel presses further. Confessing that he has nothing better to do, Ron finally agrees to attend.

The message is on repentance. Ron remains after the meeting, and asks the chaplain if God's grace ever runs out. The Chaplain explains it is more like a journey - you stumble and you get up. Ron shares that he has in the past found God's grace in jail, but he seems to lose it when he gets out. The Chaplain replies that God will never give up on you - the challenge is to not give up on yourself. He further instructs him "don't believe you have done anything that makes you unworthy in His eyes."

ANALYSIS:
1. What are your thoughts on Ron's numerous brushes with death? Why was he not making better choices?

2. How important was Nathaniel to Ron during this jail period? Do you think his outreach to invite Ron to Bible study was in any part due to Ron's helpful words to him on his first day in jail?

3. Why may Ron have been hesitant initially to attend Bible Study?

4. What kind of experience do you think Ron expected to have at Bible study? What did he actually experience?

A BUDDING AUTHOR

The scene opens on a pastor congratulating a group of inmates on their graduation from a recent Bible Study. He shares that he personally corresponds with several inmates but only with those who have the will to change. He further states that in order for that change to be successful, they must first have a plan. Ron lingers to introduce himself and asks if he would write to him. The pastor agrees and they exchange contact information.

The scene moves to Ron's cell where a library cart is making its rounds. The cart attendant randomly selects a book for Ron. It happens to be a motivational book by Rob Jolles. Later Ron decides to write to the author to share what the book meant to him. His cellmate Dwight casts doubts that someone like that would ever bother with people like them.

The camera next cuts to Rob Jolles seated in his office, looking quizzically at an envelope from the Lancaster County Prison. After reading the letter, Rob decides to write back, touched by how Ron poured out his heart to him in that letter. The two men continue to exchange letters. Rob encourages Ron to write his own book, even if Ron would be the only one to ever read it.

We see Ron diligently working on his book. Seemingly frustrated at times, he plods along. Taped on the wall in his cell is the saying Mimi often recited to him: "Good, better best, may you never rest, Until the good gets better, and the better best!"

MORAL CONCEPTS:
Perseverance is another moral concept that seems relevant here. Perseverance is defined as steadfastness in doing something despite difficulty, obstacles, discouragement or delay in achieving success. We see Ron reaching out to learn new things by reading, attending small

group bible studies and by writing to those who can be a positive influence in his life. He is embracing the very words Mimi used to speak to him so frequently.

ANALYSIS:

1. Is there a time in your life where you experienced perseverance? What was the outcome?

2. How was reaching out to Rob Jones a life changer for Ron? Is there anyone who has had a significant impact in your life?

3. Is there a story inside each of us? If you were to write one about your life, what would it say?

MIMI'S PASSING AND RON'S CHANCE

While in prison, Ron receives a phone call from his brother-in-law Gee, and learns that his mother has died. While Ron struggles to process this, Gee shares that Mimi had asked that this message be passed along to Ron: "Good better best, may you never rest; until the good gets better and the better best." Ron knows the words well, is overcome with the sorrow of this great loss and anger at himself for his foolish ways.

ANALYSIS:
1. What impact will Mimi's death will have on Ron?

2. Do you think the poem Mimi always shared with Ron was ever relevant   to him while she was alive? Do you predict it will have new meaning now?

3. Can you imagine missing your mother's funeral, because you were incarcerated? What impact would that have on your life?

A TIME FOR REFLECTION

Ron is shown on his knees, in his cell, holding his Bible. Next we see him sitting in Bible Study group considering the words of a cellmate who is sharing these verses, *"They who wait for the Lord shall renew their strength. They shall mount up with wings like eagles; they shall run and not be weary; they shall walk and not faint" (Isaiah 40:31).* The speaker shares how the chapter in Isaiah 40 sustains him.

A local congressman, attending the session is introduced. Then Ron is asked to help close the session; he nervously gets up to read. With the Chaplain's encouragement and help from Nathaniel as he struggles with a word, Ron successfully completes reading aloud - the first time since grade school!

A flashback takes us to the painful memory of his classmates laughing at his difficulty reading. The camera moves to a cracked sidewalk where we see a slowly moving stinkbug. These two images remind us not only of his early failure in reading, but of all the "cracks" in his own character where he had allowed, in his past, non-productive seeds to take hold and grow.

The scene returns to Ron, who completes the scripture reading. As the meeting breaks up, the inmate, who spoke during the meeting, hands Ron a book entitled *From Prison to Praise,* indicating that it had given him comfort in the past, and he hopes the same would be true for Ron.

ANALYSIS:

1. To what do you attribute his re-newed interest in reading, particularly his willingness to read aloud?

2. Ron has continued attending Bible Study - does he seem sincere about this?

3. What changes have you observed changes in Ron, since his mother passed?

AN UNEXPECTED IMPACT

Around this time, Kiss lands back in jail and finds out that Ron is there too. He traces him to the recreational room, thinking that Ron is probably running the joint. He is surprised to find Ron preaching to a group of prisoners. As the two men silently acknowledge one another, Ron continues his message. We see the impact upon Kiss. His thoughts keep turning to his mother and how she prayed endlessly on his behalf. At that very moment, from the pulpit Ron is sharing that "*perhaps God has us right where we are supposed to be*". As he repeats those words, we see the meaning this seems to hold for Kiss.

ANALYSIS:

1. How do you think Ron felt, seeing Kiss touched by the message he is delivering?

2. How does Ron seem different at this point in his life?

3. Does it seem that both men may begin turning in a new direction?

4. What indicators do you see that may suggest how successful they will be?

PAROLE BOARD

The scene opens with Ron, still in jail, on the phone with Rob Jolles. Ron shares he has now written over 1800 pages of his story. Rob inquires about his pending parole hearing. Understanding Ron's apprehension about it, Rob encourages him by saying that if Ron simply shares with the board the man that Rob has come to know, that he can't lose.

Soon afterward, Ron enters his parole board hearing. The board opens by sharing that there is some compelling evidence in his support from a legislator, a bestselling author, and an ex-wife with whom he has a daughter. A second member of the parole board then states, "While the record shows that a great number of people are interested in this life and this case, the person we really need to hear from right now is Mr. Ron James." *(Note: the real Ron James, making a cameo appearance in the film, is the parole board member making this statement)*

Ron (the actor) then addresses the board. He explains how he wants to dedicate his life to helping others from making the same selfish and foolish decisions he has made. He shares his remorse that his current life (as a prisoner) has little value or meaning, and that he wants to use his life in a positive way. He confirms his commitment and passion to leading a life that matters and to truly making a difference, not only in his life, but in the lives of others.

MORAL CONCEPT:
Self-Discipline is the final moral concept we will address. Its presence suggests that you serve as your own teacher, coach or trainer as well as your own disciplinarian: that you have the will within you to achieve, guide, direct and control your actions toward a certain end point. Self-discipline is at the heart of our every action whether in controlling our actions, temper or even our temptations. What we practice becomes our habit over time, and habit makes all the difference. Ron has applied

the moral concept of self-discipline while still in prison and in doing so began rebuilding his life one step at a time.

ANALYSIS

1. How important do you think self-discipline is in general to succeeding in life? What difference has it made in Ron's life? What about your own life?

2. What do you think swayed the parole board into releasing Ron? Would you have agreed with their decision? Why or why not?

3. Given his past record, do you think Ron will now stay clean?

BACK TO THE WORLD

Ron, now out of jail, is working and doing well. He has a job, a car and a place to live. He learns that Kiss is now working in a barbershop and surprises him by stopping by. Kiss shares he has been clean for several years now, and that he has never been the same since the day he walked in on Ron preaching that message in jail.

Sometime later, Ron has a chance encounter with his former cellmate, Dwight. Dwight shares that he has a daughter now and is planning her birthday party. He appears to have it all together and this gives Ron hope that he will also be successful in his re-entry into the outside world.

His joy for Dwight is short-lived. Later, while watching the news, Ron sees Dwight's picture flash on his TV screen with the caption of "Opioid Overdose at Daughter's Birthday Party."

MORAL CONCEPT:

Here we see three men's lives, two are rebuilding their lives while one has tragically lost his. Could the difference be within the choices they made and the values or morals they chose to live by? Ron has finally learned this valuable lesson and begins to lead a disciplined life. He has chosen to be lawful, and to sustain from the past addictive behaviors, no matter how strong the temptation. He has chosen to surround himself with people who inspire him to be a better man; he has developed true friendships, and he is a true friend to others. Leading a disciplined life can make all the difference in the world. Self-discipline is not simple nor easy. It requires strength, patience, practice and perseverance. But the benefits are immeasurable.

ANALYSIS:

1. What factors do you think contributed to Kiss's successful adjustment and Dwight's failure?

2. Do you think Ron's life will stay on track?

3. How important do you think a support system is to succeeding in re-entry to the outside world?

THE HELPERS THAT CAME

A friend invites Ron to attend a local meeting of Toastmasters. Ron agrees, and upon arrival is introduced to Dr Dilip, a personable and experienced speaker who is also a past President of Toastmasters International. He tells Ron that *everyone* has a story to tell, and that all that is needed is to invite the audience in and to share from the heart. Dr Dilip and Ron's friends encourage Ron to share his story that very evening.

A nervous Ron approaches the podium and shares the part of his life story about his addiction and his mother's love through it all. As he tells the story of Mimi and "Good Better Best", the audience listens attentively. He shares how he repeatedly let her down, even stooping so low as to steal her wedding ring for drug money. The honesty, humility and pain of his story moves the audience to tears. Ultimately, Ron concludes his message proclaiming that after twenty-five years of going in-and-out of prison, he finally succeeded at staying clean and drug free! With tears streaming down his face he looks up and whispers, "I did it Mom! I love you!" The audience responds with a standing ovation.

MORAL ANALYSIS:
You may be familiar with the old parable about the prodigal son, who upon taking an early inheritance from his father, lived an extravagant and carefree lifestyle. After running through all of the money he found himself penniless and resorted to rummaging for food and shelter. Realizing that even the servants in his father's home were better cared for this, he ashamedly returned home, not sure of his welcome. His father however rejoiced at his homecoming, despite the son's foolishness and poor decisions, for what truly mattered was that he had come home - - it was the relationship that was most valued, not the material goods, nor the loss of them, or the sense of failure.

ANALYSIS:

1. Can you make any comparisons to this parable and Ron's life? What about your own experiences, or someone you know?

2. What does it suggest to you about parental or family love, even when we fail to do the right things? Mimi's love was a example of this.

3. Is there someone in your life who has never given up on you? Is there someone you turn to in need?

4. Is there someone *you* have never given up on? What actions have you taken in support of them?

PAROLE FREE

The scene returns to Ron and Rick in the parole office and Ron says, "That's the story, Rick." Rick shares his amazement at how it all turned out, and that someone must have really been watching over him. Ron glances upward, thinking of Mimi, and agrees.

As Ron leaves the office, he sees a brief faded *vision of Maggie May,* now old and haggard, beckoning him. He pauses for a moment, and chooses to ignore this with the confidence that "she" (i.e. drugs) will no longer have a hold on him. With surety and peace of mind, he walks forward to a car that is waiting for him. That car, and everything in it, represents the new life that Ron has built. At the wheel is his new wife Annie, and as the camera pans to the back seat we see their infant daughter. His drug-dependent days are over. He is now, today, a productive member of society: a dedicated Christ follower, a responsible and loving husband and father, an accomplished salesmen, businessman, author, and speaker who travels across the country with a vivid and compelling message to young people.

MORAL CONCEPTS:
Courage is the final moral value we'll discuss. Webster defines it as the mental or moral strength to persevere and withstand danger, fear or difficulty. Certainly these are obstacles Ron has overcome in his life. Others define courage as the ability to do something that frightens oneself, or that requires strength in the face of pain or grief. In Ron's case, perhaps this best sums it up: to have the courage of one's convictions, to act in accordance with one's beliefs. Having the courage to do the right thing is one thing, but it requires wisdom to know what the right thing is! And wisdom is what we obtain when we learn the lessons of all of the moral concepts we have been reviewing in this workbook. Think about them, practice them and make them a part of your life, if they are not already present. And along the way, pause to help others in their journey.

ANALYSIS:

1. How would you describe Mimi's love for Ron?

2. What do you think it symbolizes when Ron sees and walks past *an image* of a faded haggard "Maggie Mae" as he leaves his final parole meeting with Rick?

3. What is your prediction about how successful Ron will be in remaining drug free at this point in his life?

CONCLUSION

How will the things you have learned through Ron's life impact your life ?

What might you change in your life?

What choices will you make?

My struggles through the ups and downs of drug addiction were epic. The fact that I was able to make it through has a lot to do with my renewed faith and belief in a higher power and I would like to make that very clear.

I have come to understand that our purpose in life is not to live selfishly for ourselves, but to live responsibly in a mature, lawful and productive manner. We are to be responsible in our actions, and to conduct ourselves with self-discipline and to go about our work with honesty and dignity. We are to demonstrate courage and perseverance in the face of adversity and temptation, and above all we are to be thoughtful in our deeds, give of ourselves to others and to show compassion for others. These are the morals I strive to live by today.

The ultimate thing is gaining wisdom. Whether it comes by reading, studying independently, within small group studies, or by surrounding yourself with good friends and great role models, always seek wisdom and choose to be a life-long learner. By gaining wisdom and experiencing a change of heart it becomes easier and more natural to become law-abiding and to live righteously.

At the end of the day, the most important "choice" I made was to examine and further develop my own faith in spiritual matters. This is what is responsible for the man I am today. It is my sincere wish that you consider a similar examination and explore the difference it may make in your own life. In closing, I wish you the courage to always make wise choices.

Remain blessed.

Ron L. James

AVAILABLE NOW

Retail: $23.95
ISBN: 978-1-945169-07-6

Choices is a compelling, inspirational autobiography that shares life-changing wisdom for anyone who wants to begin making better choices today. James chronicles the bad choices he made which resulted in personal cost and tragic results. His journey is a thought-provoking account beginning from a young age through his downward spiral which ultimately landed him in a nine-by-nine cell for over 25 years. James encourages and empowers others to learn from his mistakes. He challenges them to consider their choices and trust in God to experience a life greater than ever imagined. As you read *Choices*, you will discover the same truth James discovered. Choices determine destiny.

Have you ever faced a situation or a problem that was monumental in your life? Instead of running away or giving up. You make the choice to meet that challenge head-on and after countless hours and hard work, you find yourself victorious! That's what "Living in your Next Choice" is all about. It's the resolve of what life is all about after you've made a wise choice. Now—what will you do with your next Choice?

Retail: $10.95
ISBN: 978-1-945169-08-3

Choices Workbook Available—Retail $11
Choices Bible Study Available—Retail $11

NEW RELEASE

CHOICES, The Movie

Please visit our website to learn more about the movie and connect with us on social media to receive updates.

www.ChoicesMovie.com

Your Choice Foundation's goal is to inspire individuals to build on their gifts to empower others.

Please send your support for this mission to:

Your Choice Foundation
1245 W Princess St., York, PA 17404
717-850-3538

www.YourChoiceFoundation.org

www.ingramcontent.com/pod-product-compliance
Lightning Source LLC
Chambersburg PA
CBHW071536080526
44588CB00011B/1679